A GIFT FOR:

Don Pape

BY:

Stephen Leaders

God's Promises for Your Life

Published by Thomas Nelson, Inc.

The Parable Group
3563 Empleo Street
San Luis Obispo, CA 93401

Cover and interior designed by Robin Black, Blackbird Creative, LLC, www.blackbirdcreative.biz
Original package design © 2006 Thomas Nelson, Inc.

ISBN–10: 1-4041-8688-3
ISBN–13: 978-14041-8688-0

Printed in Mexico

Let us hold fast
the confession of our faith
without wavering, for
He who promised is faithful.

HEBREWS 10:23

TABLE OF CONTENTS

WHAT IT MEANS TO LIVE FOR JESUS CHRIST

When you accept Jesus Christ as your personal Savior, it is the beginning of a new journey that will change your life and fill you with a certain peace that passes all understanding. God has promised through His Word that when you accept Jesus Christ, you are "a new creation; old things are passed away; behold, all things have become new" (2 Corinthians 5:17). From this day forward you belong to the family of God, your sins are forgiven, and God accepts you just as you are.

As you go forward in life, our prayer is that you will take the necessary steps to discover God's plan and purpose for you. His promises are sure, and you can depend on God to guide your whole life if you will trust Him with your spiritual life. Proverbs 3:5-6 says:

"Trust in the LORD with all your heart,
And lean not on your own understanding;
In all your ways acknowledge Him,
And He shall direct your paths."

What God has promised in His Word, you can count on in your life.

Some important things to realize when you become a Christian are that God wants to become involved in the way you walk, talk, think, and live. With Jesus Christ now living inside you, God has freed you from the penalty of your past sins. As you obey God's commandments and apply the principles of God's Word to your daily life, your attitude and priorities will change, and as the transformation continues and you allow Jesus Christ to be the Lord of your life, you will become more and more like Him every day.

Your relationship with God has nothing to do with your being good enough, but it is available only because Jesus Christ died on the cross for you. Through Him your sins are forgiven. God has an entirely new blessed life for you. He has forgiven your past and has prepared a future filled with His love and abundance—BELIEVE IT AND RECEIVE IT!

Holy Spirit

God's gift to each Christian is the Holy Spirit, to live in our hearts and be our comforter, our Teacher, our Helper and our Guide. You are given the Holy Spirit to help you be strong and continually break any hindrance in your life. The power of the Holy Spirit is promised to you in Acts 1:8: "you shall receive power when the Holy Spirit has come upon you." This power is one of God's many gifts to you, and all you have to do is receive the Holy Spirit.

Scripture

The Word of God is food to your spirit. The more you read and apply God's Word to your life, the more you will grow spiritually. Psalm 119:105 says, "Your word is a lamp to my feet and a light to my path." The Bible is the inspired word of God. Second Timothy 3:16-17 says, "All Scripture is given by inspiration of God and is profitable for doctrine, for reproof, for correction, for inspiration in righteousness, that the man of God may be complete, thoroughly equipped for every good work."

God's Word is a road map to live a successful life. Set aside some time every day to read it. Start with the gospels, particularly John and Mark. Ask God to help you understand each verse and the wealth of wisdom contained in His Word. This little book you're holding now can help you discover many of God's promises contained in the Bible and can help you learn to depend on His Word for daily guidance.

Prayer

As you have been encouraged to read your Bible every day, you also should develop the habit of coming to God in prayer. He is after all, your loving heavenly Father who yearns to interact with you and listen as you open your heart to Him. The key to a fruitful prayer life is spending time abiding with Jesus and His teaching. John 15:7 says, "If you abide in Me and My words abide in you, you will ask what you desire, and it shall be done for you."

Praying is as important to your life as breathing, and as you talk to God—and listen to Him—He responds to you. Talk to God often. Tell Him about your challenges, successes, failures, struggles, and feelings. As you praise Him and thank Him for His love, He will guide you and bless you. If you make prayer a daily habit, you will discover that the experience can change your life.

Church

Because you have accepted Jesus Christ as your personal Savior, you now belong to His family, the church. It is very important that you find a good Bible-teaching church to attend regularly as soon as possible. As you grow as a Christian, the gifts and talents that the Lord has given to you will be a great blessing to the church. You also will be blessed and encouraged through the mentoring and association with other believers. Therefore, choose a church where the Word of God is preached and Jesus Christ is lifted up as Savior and Lord.

Daily Life

God wants you to grow in faith and share with others what Jesus Christ means to you. On the following pages of this book you will find God's promises taken from Scripture and topically oriented to address everyday needs. God loves you and wants you to have victory in every area of your life. He will help you, lead you, and prepare you for a purposeful life for His glory. In John 10:10 Jesus declares, "I have come that [you] may have life and that [you] may have it more abundantly."

Give God your best for the rest of your life.

Add to your faith virtue, to virtue,
knowledge, to knowledge self-control,
to self-control, perseverance,
to perseverance godliness,
to godliness brotherly kindness,
and to brotherly kindness love.
For if these things are yours and abound,
you will be neither barren nor unfruitful in the
knowledge of our Lord Jesus Christ.

2 PETER 1:5-8

God's Promises for When You Need. . .

Courage

Wait on the LORD;
Be of good courage,
And He shall strengthen your heart;
Wait, I say, on the LORD!

PSALM 27:14

Beloved, do not think it strange
concerning the fiery trial which is to try you,
as though some strange thing happened to you;
but rejoice to the extent that you partake
of Christ's sufferings, that when His glory is revealed,
you may also be glad with exceeding joy.

1 PETER 4:12–13

For I am persuaded that neither death nor life, nor angels nor principalities nor powers, nor things present nor things to come, nor height nor depth, nor any other created thing, shall be able to separate us from the love of God which is in Christ Jesus our Lord.

ROMANS 8:38–39

Courage

Fear not, for I am with you;
Be not dismayed, for I am your God.
I will strengthen you,
Yes, I will help you,
I will uphold you with My righteous right hand.

ISAIAH 41:10

But those who wait on the LORD
Shall renew their strength;
They shall mount up with wings like eagles,
They shall run and not be weary,
They shall walk and not faint.

ISAIAH 40:31

Be of good courage,
And He shall strengthen your heart,
All you who hope in the LORD.

PSALM 31:24

I can do all things through Christ who strengthens me.

PHILIPPIANS 4:13

Knowing that the testing of your faith produces patience. But let patience have its perfect work, that you may be perfect and complete, lacking nothing.

JAMES 1:3–4

The end of a thing is better than its beginning;
The patient in spirit is better than the proud in spirit.
Do not hasten in your spirit to be angry,
For anger rests in the bosom of fools.

ECCLESIASTES 7:8–9

For whatever things were written before were written for our learning, that we through the patience and comfort of the Scriptures might have hope. Now may the God of patience and comfort grant you to be like-minded toward one another, according to Christ Jesus.

ROMANS 15:4–5

Rest in the LORD, and wait patiently for Him;
Do not fret because of him who prospers in his way,
Because of the man who brings wicked schemes to pass.

PSALM 37:7

Therefore do not cast away your confidence, which has great reward. For you have need of endurance, so that after you have done the will of God, you may receive the promise:
"For yet a little while,
And He who is coming will come and will not tarry."

HEBREWS 10:35–37

And not only that, but we also glory in tribulations, knowing that tribulation produces perseverance; and perseverance, character; and character, hope. Now hope does not disappoint, because the love of God has been poured out in our hearts by the Holy Spirit who was given to us.

ROMANS 5:3–5

Peace

Be anxious for nothing, but in everything by prayer and supplication, with thanksgiving, let your requests be made known to God; and the peace of God, which surpasses all understanding, will guard your hearts and minds through Christ Jesus.

PHILIPPIANS 4:6–7

You will keep him in perfect peace,
Whose mind is stayed on You,
Because he trusts in You.

ISAIAH 26:3

Now may the Lord of peace Himself give you peace always in every way. The Lord be with you all.

2 THESSALONIANS 3:16

Peace I leave with you, My peace I give to you;
not as the world gives do I give to you.
Let not your heart be troubled,
neither let it be afraid.

JOHN 14:27

Comfort

Sing, O heavens!
Be joyful, O earth!
And break out in singing, O mountains!
For the LORD has comforted His people,
And will have mercy on His afflicted.

ISAIAH 49:13

Blessed be the God and Father of our Lord Jesus Christ, the Father of mercies and God of all comfort, who comforts us in all our tribulation, that we may be able to comfort those who are in any trouble, with the comfort with which we ourselves are comforted by God.

2 CORINTHIANS 1:3–4

Yea, though I walk through
the valley of the shadow of death,
I will fear no evil;
For You are with me;
Your rod and Your staff, they comfort me.

PSALM 23:4

Comfort

Fear not, for I am with you;
Be not dismayed, for I am your God.
I will strengthen you,
Yes, I will help you,
I will uphold you with My righteous right hand.

ISAIAH 41:10

"For the eyes of the LORD are on the righteous,
And His ears are open to their prayers;
But the face of the LORD is against those who do evil."
And who is he who will harm you
if you become followers of what is good?

1 PETER 3:12–13

Behold, I am the LORD, the God of all flesh.
Is there anything too hard for Me?

JEREMIAH 32:27

Assurance

So Jesus answered and said to them,
"Have faith in God. For assuredly, I say to you,
whoever says to this mountain, 'Be removed and be cast
into the sea,' and does not doubt in his heart,
but believes that those things he says will be done,
he will have whatever he says. Therefore I say to you,
whatever things you ask when you pray,
believe that you receive them,
and you will have them."

MARK 11:22–24

The Lord is not slack concerning His promise,
as some count slackness, but is longsuffering toward us,
not willing that any should perish
but that all should come to repentance.

2 PETER 3:9

As for God, His way is perfect;
The word of the LORD is proven;
He is a shield to all who trust in Him.

PSALM 18:30

Assurance

Behold, the LORD's hand is not shortened,
That it cannot save;
Nor His ear heavy,
That it cannot hear.

ISAIAH 59:1

And do not seek what you should eat
or what you should drink, nor have an anxious mind.
For all these things the nations of the world
seek after, and your Father knows that you need these
things. But seek the kingdom of God,
and all these things shall be added to you.

LUKE 12:29–31

He did not waver at the promise of God
through unbelief, but was strengthened in faith,
giving glory to God, and being fully convinced that
what He had promised He was also able to perform.

ROMANS 4:20–21

Confidence

I can do all things through Christ
who strengthens me.

PHILIPPIANS 4:13

Therefore do not cast away your confidence,
which has great reward. For you have need of endurance,
so that after you have done the will of God,
you may receive the promise.

HEBREWS 10:35–36

Being confident of this very thing,
that He who has begun a good work in you
will complete it until the day of Jesus Christ.

PHILIPPIANS 1:6

The LORD God is my strength;
He will make my feet like deer's feet,
And He will make me walk on my high hills.

HABAKKUK 3:19

GOD'S PROMISES FOR WHEN YOU NEED . . .

Confidence

Yet in all these things we are more than conquerors
through Him who loved us.

ROMANS 8:37

Now this is the confidence that we have in Him,
that if we ask anything according to His will,
He hears us. And if we know that He hears us,
whatever we ask, we know that
we have the petitions that we have asked of Him.

1 JOHN 5:14–15

Most assuredly, I say to you,
he who believes in Me,
the works that I do he will do also;
and greater works than these he will do,
because I go to My Father.

JOHN 14:12

For the LORD will be your confidence,
And will keep your foot from being caught.

PROVERBS 3:26

Faith

Now faith is the substance of things hoped for,
the evidence of things not seen.

HEBREWS 11:1

So then faith comes by hearing,
and hearing by the word of God.

ROMANS 10:17

But without faith it is impossible to please Him,
for he who comes to God must believe
that He is, and that He is a rewarder
of those who diligently seek Him.

HEBREWS 11:6

Jesus said to him, "If you can believe, all things
are possible to him who believes."

MARK 9:23

Faith

For whatever is born of God overcomes the world.
And this is the victory that
has overcome the world—our faith.

1 JOHN 5:4

That the genuineness of your faith,
being much more precious than gold that perishes,
though it is tested by fire, may be found to praise,
honor, and glory at the revelation of Jesus Christ,
whom having not seen you love. Though now
you do not see Him, yet believing,
you rejoice with joy inexpressible and full of glory,
receiving the end of your faith—
the salvation of your souls.

1 PETER 1:7–9

So the Lord said, "If you have faith as a mustard seed,
you can say to this mulberry tree,
'Be pulled up by the roots and be planted
in the sea,' and it would obey you."

LUKE 17:6

Love

Though I speak with the tongues of men and of angels,
but have not love, I have become sounding
brass or a clanging cymbal. And though I have the gift
of prophecy, and understand all mysteries and all
knowledge, and though I have all faith, so that I could
remove mountains, but have not love, I am nothing.
And though I bestow all my goods to feed
the poor, and though I give my body to be burned,
but have not love, it profits me nothing.
Love suffers long and is kind; love does not envy;
love does not parade itself, is not puffed up; does not
behave rudely, does not seek its own, is not provoked,
thinks no evil; does not rejoice in iniquity,
but rejoices in the truth; bears all things,
believes all things, hopes all things, endures all things.
Love never fails. But whether there are prophecies,
they will fail; whether there are tongues, they will cease;
whether there is knowledge, it will vanish away. . . .
And now abide faith, hope, love, these three;
but the greatest of these is love.

1 CORINTHIANS 13:1–8, 13

Love

Beloved, let us love one another,
for love is of God; and everyone who loves is
born of God and knows God. Be who does not love
does not know God, for God is love.

1 JOHN 4:7–8

As the Father loved Me, I also have loved you;
abide in My love. If you keep My commandments,
you will abide in My love, just as I have kept
My Father's commandments and abide in His love.

JOHN 15:9–10

The LORD has appeared of old to me, saying:
"Yes, I have loved you with an everlasting love;
Therefore with lovingkindness I have drawn you."

JEREMIAH 31:3

For God so loved the world that He gave His only
begotten Son, that whoever believes in Him should
not perish but have everlasting life.

JOHN 3:16

Love

For I am persuaded that neither death nor life,
nor angels nor principalities nor powers,
nor things present nor things to come, nor height nor depth, nor any other created thing, shall be able to separate us from the love of God which is in Christ Jesus our Lord.

ROMANS 8:38–39

In this is love, not that we loved God,
but that He loved us and sent His Son to be the propitiation for our sins. Beloved, if God so loved us, we also ought to love one another. No one has seen God at any time. If we love one another, God abides in us, and His love has been perfected in us.

1 JOHN 4:10–12

I love those who love me,
And those who seek me diligently will find me.

PROVERBS 8:17

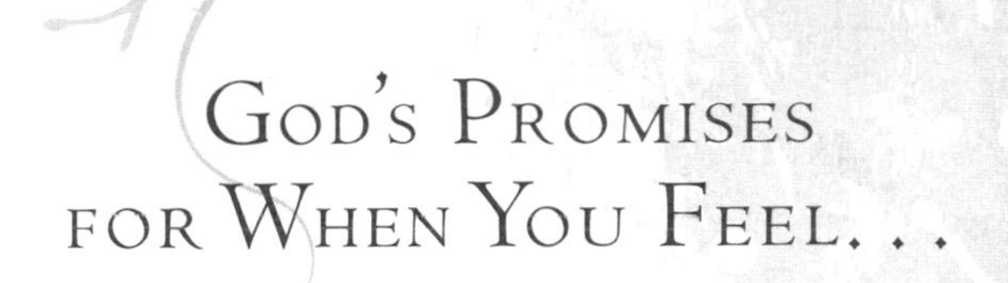

God's Promises for When You Feel. . .

Dissatisfied

The young lions lack and suffer hunger;
But those who seek the LORD shall
not lack any good thing.

PSALM 34:10

O God, You are my God;
Early will I seek You;
My soul thirsts for You;
My flesh longs for You
In a dry and thirsty land
Where there is no water.
So I have looked for You in the sanctuary,
To see Your power and Your glory.
Because Your lovingkindness is better than life,
My lips shall praise You.
Thus I will bless You while I live;
I will lift up my hands in Your name.
My soul shall be satisfied as with marrow and fatness,
And my mouth shall praise You with joyful lips.

PSALM 63:1–5

Dissatisfied

Blessed are those who hunger and thirst
for righteousness,
For they shall be filled.

MATTHEW 5:6

And God is able to make all grace abound toward you,
that you, always having all sufficiency in all things,
may have an abundance for every good work.

2 CORINTHIANS 9:8

Bless the LORD, O my soul,
And forget not all His benefits.

PSALM 103:2–5

Who forgives all your iniquities,
Who heals all your diseases,
Who redeems your life from destruction,
Who crowns you with lovingkindness
and tender mercies,
Who satisfies your mouth with good things,
So that your youth is renewed like the eagle's.

PSALM 103:2–5

Dissatisfied

Not that I speak in regard to need, for I have
learned in whatever state I am, to be content:
I know how to be abased, and I know how to abound.
Everywhere and in all things I have learned
both to be full and to be hungry,
both to abound and to suffer need. I can do all
things through Christ who strengthens me.

PHILIPPIANS 4:11–13

Oh, that men would give thanks to the LORD
for His goodness,
And for His wonderful works to the children of men!
For He satisfies the longing soul,
And fills the hungry soul with goodness.

PSALM 107:8–9

Confused

For God is not the author of confusion but of peace,
as in all the churches of the saints.

1 CORINTHIANS 14:33

For God has not given us a spirit of fear,
but of power and of love and of a sound mind.

2 TIMOTHY 1:7

For where envy and self-seeking exist,
confusion and every evil thing are there.
But the wisdom that is from above is first pure,
then peaceable, gentle, willing to yield, full of mercy and
good fruits, without partiality and without hypocrisy.
Now the fruit of righteousness is
sown in peace by those who make peace.

JAMES 3:16–18

Confused

If any of you lacks wisdom,
let him ask of God, who gives to all liberally
and without reproach,
and it will be given to him.

JAMES 1:5

Trust in the LORD with all your heart,
And lean not on your own understanding;
In all your ways acknowledge Him,
And He shall direct your paths.

PROVERBS 3:5–6

Cast your burden on the LORD,
And He shall sustain you;
He shall never permit the righteous to be moved.

PSALM 55:22

Discouraged

In this you greatly rejoice, though now for a little while,
if need be, you have been grieved by various trials,
that the genuineness of your faith,
being much more precious than gold that perishes,
though it is tested by fire, may be found to praise,
honor, and glory at the revelation of Jesus Christ, whom
having not seen you love. Though now you
do not see Him, yet believing, you rejoice with joy
inexpressible and full of glory, receiving the
end of your faith—the salvation of your souls.

1 PETER 1:6–9

Let not your heart be troubled;
you believe in God, believe also in Me.

JOHN 14:1

Though I walk in the midst of trouble,
You will revive me;
You will stretch out Your hand
Against the wrath of my enemies,
And Your right hand will save me.

PSALM 138:7

Discouraged

The LORD is my light and my salvation;
Whom shall I fear?
The LORD is the strength of my life;
Of whom shall I be afraid?
When the wicked came against me
To eat up my flesh,
My enemies and foes,
They stumbled and fell.
Though an army may encamp against me,
My heart shall not fear;
Though war may rise against me,
In this I will be confident.

PSALM 27:1–3

Be anxious for nothing, but in everything by prayer and supplication, with thanksgiving, let your requests be made known to God; and the peace of God, which surpasses all understanding, will guard your hearts and minds through Christ Jesus.

PHILIPPIANS 4:6–7

Lonely

Let your conduct be without covetousness;
be content with such things as you have.
For He Himself has said,
"I will never leave you nor forsake you."

HEBREWS 13:5

"Teaching them to observe all things that
I have commanded you; and lo, I am with you always,
even to the end of the age." Amen.

MATTHEW 28:20

Fear not, for I am with you;
Be not dismayed, for I am your God.
I will strengthen you,
Yes, I will help you,
I will uphold you with My righteous right hand.

ISAIAH 41:10

Be strong and of good courage, do not fear nor be afraid
of them; for the LORD your God, He is the One
who goes with you. He will not leave you nor forsake you.

DEUTERONOMY 31:6

Lonely

"For the mountains shall depart
And the hills be removed,
But My kindness shall not depart from you,
Nor shall My covenant of peace be removed,"
Says the LORD, who has mercy on you.

ISAIAH 54:10

Casting all your care upon Him,
for He cares for you.

1 PETER 5:7

God is our refuge and strength,
A very present help in trouble.

PSALM 46:1

The LORD will not forsake His people, for His great
name's sake, because it has pleased the
LORD to make you His people.

1 SAMUEL 12:22

Depressed

The righteous cry out, and the LORD hears,
And delivers them out of all their troubles.

PSALM 34:17

Beloved, do not think it strange
concerning the fiery trial which is to try you,
as though some strange thing happened to you; but
rejoice to the extent that you partake of Christ's
sufferings, that when His glory is revealed,
you may also be glad with exceeding joy.

1 PETER 4:12–13

Blessed be the God and Father of our Lord Jesus
Christ, the Father of mercies and God of all comfort,
who comforts us in all our tribulation,
that we may be able to comfort those who are in
any trouble, with the comfort with which
we ourselves are comforted by God.

2 CORINTHIANS 1:3–4

Depressed

Finally, brethren, whatever things are true,
whatever things are noble, whatever things are just,
whatever things are pure, whatever things
are lovely, whatever things are of good report, if there is
any virtue and if there is anything praiseworthy—
meditate on these things.

PHILIPPIANS 4:8

He heals the brokenhearted
And binds up their wounds.

PSALM 147:3

For His anger is but for a moment,
His favor is for life;
Weeping may endure for a night,
But joy comes in the morning.

PSALM 30:5

Angry

So then, my beloved brethren, let every man be swift to hear, slow to speak, slow to wrath; for the wrath of man does not produce the righteousness of God.

JAMES 1:19–20

"Be angry, and do not sin":
do not let the sun go down on your wrath.

EPHESIANS 4:26

For if you forgive men their trespasses,
your heavenly Father will also forgive you.

MATTHEW 6:14

He who is slow to wrath has great understanding,
But he who is impulsive exalts folly.

PROVERBS 14:29

He who is slow to anger is better than the mighty,
And he who rules his spirit than he who takes a city.

PROVERBS 16:32

Angry

Beloved, do not avenge yourselves,
but rather give place to wrath; for it is written,
"Vengeance is Mine, I will repay," says the Lord.

ROMANS 12:19

If your enemy is hungry, give him bread to eat;
And if he is thirsty, give him water to drink;
For so you will heap coals of fire on his head,
And the LORD will reward you.

PROVERBS 25:21–22

Let all bitterness, wrath, anger, clamor,
and evil speaking be put away from you, with all malice.
And be kind to one another, tenderhearted, forgiving
one another, even as God in Christ forgave you.

EPHESIANS 4:31–32

Worried

And let the peace of God rule in your hearts, to which also you were called in one body; and be thankful.

COLOSSIANS 3:15

For to be carnally minded is death,
but to be spiritually minded is life and peace.

ROMANS 8:6

Be anxious for nothing, but in everything by prayer and supplication, with thanksgiving, let your requests be made known to God; and the peace of God, which surpasses all understanding, will guard your hearts and minds through Christ Jesus.

PHILIPPIANS 4:6–7

You will keep him in perfect peace,
Whose mind is stayed on You,
Because he trusts in You.

ISAIAH 26:3

And my God shall supply all your need
according to His riches in glory by Christ Jesus.

PHILIPPIANS 4:19

Worried

Therefore I say to you, do not worry about your life,
what you will eat or what you will drink;
nor about your body, what you will put on.
Is not life more than food and the body more than
clothing? Look at the birds of the air, for they neither
sow nor reap nor gather into barns; yet your
heavenly Father feeds them. Are you not of more value
than they? Which of you by worrying can add one
cubit to his stature? So why do you worry about clothing?
Consider the lilies of the field, how they grow:
they neither toil nor spin; and yet I say to you that even
Solomon in all his glory was not arrayed like one
of these. Now if God so clothes the grass of the field,
which today is, and tomorrow is thrown into
the oven, will He not much more clothe you,
O you of little faith? Therefore do not worry, saying,
"What shall we eat?" or "What shall we drink?"
or "What shall we wear?" For after all these things the
Gentiles seek. For your heavenly Father knows
that you need all these things.

MATTHEW 6:25–32

Tempted

Therefore let him who thinks he stands take heed lest he fall. No temptation has overtaken you except such as is common to man; but God is faithful, who will not allow you to be tempted beyond what you are able, but with the temptation will also make the way of escape, that you may be able to bear it.

1 CORINTHIANS 10:12–13

Seeing then that we have a great High Priest who has passed through the heavens, Jesus the Son of God, let us hold fast our confession. For we do not have a High Priest who cannot sympathize with our weaknesses, but was in all points tempted as we are, yet without sin. Let us therefore come boldly to the throne of grace, that we may obtain mercy and find grace to help in time of need.

HEBREWS 4:14–16

Then the Lord knows how to deliver the godly out of temptations and to reserve the unjust under punishment for the day of judgment.

2 PETER 2:9

Tempted

Let no one say when he is tempted, "I am tempted by God"; for God cannot be tempted by evil, nor does He Himself tempt anyone. But each one is tempted when he is drawn away by his own desires and enticed.

JAMES 1:13–14

Be sober, be vigilant; because your adversary the devil walks about like a roaring lion, seeking whom he may devour. Resist him, steadfast in the faith, knowing that the same sufferings are experienced by your brotherhood in the world.

1 PETER 5:8–9

Finally, my brethren, be strong in the Lord and in the power of His might. Put on the whole armor of God, that you may be able to stand against the wiles of the devil . . . above all, taking the shield of faith with which you will be able to quench all the fiery darts of the wicked one.

EPHESIANS 6:10–11, 16

Tempted

Therefore submit to God.
Resist the devil and he will flee from you.

JAMES 4:7

Blessed is the man who endures temptation;
for when he has been approved,
he will receive the crown of life which the Lord
has promised to those who love Him.

JAMES 1:12

In that He Himself has suffered, being tempted,
He is able to aid those who are tempted.

HEBREWS 2:18

Behold, God is mighty, but despises no one;
He is mighty in strength of understanding.

JOB 36:5

But the salvation of the righteous is from the LORD;
He is their strength in the time of trouble.

PSALM 37:39

God's Promises that Jesus Is Your. . .

Companion

A man who has friends must himself be friendly,
But there is a friend who sticks closer than a brother.

PROVERBS 18:24

Let your conduct be without covetousness;
be content with such things as you have.
For He Himself has said,
"I will never leave you nor forsake you."

HEBREWS 13:5

No longer do I call you servants, for a servant
does not know what his master is doing;
but I have called you friends, for all things that I heard
from My Father I have made known to you.
You did not choose Me, but I chose you and appointed
you that you should go and bear fruit,
and that your fruit should remain, that whatever you
ask the Father in My name He may give you.

JOHN 15:15–16

Companion

Draw near to God and He will draw near to you.
Cleanse your hands, you sinners;
and purify your hearts, you double–minded.

JAMES 4:8

"For the mountains shall depart
And the hills be removed,
But My kindness shall not depart from you,
Nor shall My covenant of peace be removed,"
Says the LORD, who has mercy on you.

ISAIAH 54:10

When my father and my mother forsake me,
Then the LORD will take care of me.

PSALM 27:10

Savior

Not by works of righteousness which we have done,
but according to His mercy He saved us,
through the washing of regeneration and renewing
of the Holy Spirit, whom He poured out
on us abundantly through Jesus Christ our Savior.

TITUS 3:5–6

For God so loved the world that He gave His
only begotten Son, that whoever believes in Him
should not perish but have everlasting life.

JOHN 3:16

That if you confess with your mouth the
Lord Jesus and believe in your heart that God has
raised Him from the dead, you will be saved.

ROMANS 10:9

Therefore, if anyone is in Christ,
he is a new creation; old things have passed away;
behold, all things have become new.

2 CORINTHIANS 5:17

GOD'S PROMISES THAT JESUS IS YOUR . . . *Savior*

Being justified freely by His grace
through the redemption that is in Christ Jesus,
whom God set forth as a propitiation by His blood,
through faith, to demonstrate His righteousness,
because in His forbearance God had passed over the
sins that were previously committed.

ROMANS 3:24–25

But God, who is rich in mercy, because of His great
love with which He loved us, even when we were
dead in trespasses, made us alive together
with Christ (by grace you have been saved). . . .
For by grace you have been saved through faith,
and that not of yourselves; it is the gift of God,
not of works, lest anyone should boast.

EPHESIANS 2:4–5, 8–9

Who has saved us and called us with a holy calling,
not according to our works, but according to
His own purpose and grace which was given to us
in Christ Jesus before time began.

2 TIMOTHY 1:9

Deliverer

"And you shall know the truth,
and the truth shall make you free." . . . Therefore if the
Son makes you free, you shall be free indeed.

JOHN 8:32, 36

Now the Lord is the Spirit; and where the
Spirit of the Lord is, there is liberty.

2 CORINTHIANS 3:17

But now having been set free from sin,
and having become slaves of God, you have your fruit
to holiness, and the end, everlasting life.

ROMANS 6:22

And these signs will follow those who believe:
In My name they will cast out demons;
they will speak with new tongues.

MARK 16:17

For the law of the Spirit of life
in Christ Jesus has made me free from
the law of sin and death.

ROMANS 8:2

The Spirit of the Lord GOD is upon Me,
Because the LORD has anointed Me
To preach good tidings to the poor;
He has sent Me to heal the brokenhearted,
To proclaim liberty to the captives,
And the opening of the prison to those who are bound.

ISAIAH 61:1

For He will deliver the needy when he cries,
The poor also, and him who has no helper.

PSALM 72:12

Example

For to this you were called,
because Christ also suffered for us, leaving us an
example, that you should follow His steps.

1 PETER 2:21

If I then, your Lord and Teacher,
have washed your feet, you also ought to wash one
another's feet. For I have given you an example,
that you should do as I have done to you.

JOHN 13:14–15

Let this mind be in you which was also in Christ Jesus,
who, being in the form of God, did not consider
it robbery to be equal with God, but made Himself of
no reputation, taking the form of a bondservant,
and coming in the likeness of men. And being found in
appearance as a man, He humbled Himself and
became obedient to the point of death,
even the death of the cross.

PHILIPPIANS 2:5–8

Example

Yet it shall not be so among you;
but whoever desires to become great among you shall be your servant. And whoever of you desires to be first shall be slave of all. For even the Son of Man did not come to be served, but to serve, and to give His life a ransom for many.

MARK 10:43–45

A new commandment I give to you, that you love one another; as I have loved you, that you also love one another.

JOHN 13:34

Now may the God of patience and comfort grant you to be like-minded toward one another, according to Christ Jesus, that you may with one mind and one mouth glorify the God and Father of our Lord Jesus Christ. Therefore receive one another, just as Christ also received us, to the glory of God.

ROMANS 15:5–7

Example

And you know that He was manifested
to take away our sins, and in Him there is no sin.
Whoever abides in Him does not sin.
Whoever sins has neither seen Him nor known Him.
Little children, let no one deceive you. He who practices
righteousness is righteous, just as He is righteous.

1 JOHN 3:5–7

When He had called the people to Himself,
with His disciples also, He said to them,
"Whoever desires to come after Me,
let him deny himself,
and take up his cross,
and follow Me."

MARK 8:34

Therefore be imitators of God as dear children.
And walk in love as Christ also has loved us and
given Himself for us, an offering and a sacrifice
to God for a sweet-smelling aroma.

EPHESIANS 5:1-2

GOD'S PROMISES THAT JESUS IS YOUR . . .

Guardian

He will not cry out, nor raise His voice,
Nor cause His voice to be heard in the street.

ISAIAH 42:2

But You, O LORD, are a shield for me,
My glory and the One who lifts up my head.

PSALM 3:3

The LORD your God in your midst,
The Mighty One, will save;
He will rejoice over you with gladness,
He will quiet you with His love,
He will rejoice over you with singing.

ZEPHANIAH 3:17

A thousand may fall at your side,
And ten thousand at your right hand;
But it shall not come near you.

PSALM 91:7

Guardian

"For the eyes of the LORD are on the righteous,
And His ears are open to their prayers;
But the face of the LORD is against those who do evil."
And who is he who will harm you if you become
followers of what is good?

1 PETER 3:12–13

The eternal God is your refuge,
And underneath are the everlasting arms;
He will thrust out the enemy from before you,
And will say, "Destroy!"

DEUTERONOMY 33:27

The LORD bless you and keep you;
The LORD make His face shine upon you,
And be gracious to you;
The LORD lift up His countenance upon you,
And give you peace.

NUMBERS 6:24-26

Security

Blessed be the God and Father of our
Lord Jesus Christ, who according to His abundant
mercy has begotten us again to a living hope through
the resurrection of Jesus Christ from the dead,
to an inheritance incorruptible and undefiled and that
does not fade away, reserved in heaven for you,
who are kept by the power of God through faith for
salvation ready to be revealed in the last time.

1 PETER 1:3–5

My sheep hear My voice, and I know them,
and they follow Me. And I give them eternal life, and
they shall never perish; neither shall anyone
snatch them out of My hand. My Father, who has given
them to Me, is greater than all; and no one is able
to snatch them out of My Father's hand.

JOHN 10:27–29

Being confident of this very thing,
that He who has begun a good work in you
will complete it until the day of Jesus Christ.

PHILIPPIANS 1:6

Security

For I am persuaded that neither death nor life, nor angels nor principalities nor powers, nor things present nor things to come, nor height nor depth, nor any other created thing, shall be able to separate us from the love of God which is in Christ Jesus our Lord.

ROMANS 8:38–39

Now to Him who is able to keep you from stumbling,
And to present you faultless
Before the presence of His glory with exceeding joy,
To God our Savior,
Who alone is wise,
Be glory and majesty,
Dominion and power,
Both now and forever.
Amen.

JUDE 1:24–25

Security

Lift up your eyes on high,
And see who has created these things,
Who brings out their host by number;
He calls them all by name,
By the greatness of His might
And the strength of His power;
Not one is missing.

ISAIAH 40:26

In Him you also trusted, after you heard the word of truth, the gospel of your salvation; in whom also, having believed, you were sealed with the Holy Spirit of promise.

EPHESIANS 1:13

Surely goodness and mercy shall follow me
All the days of my life;
And I will dwell in the house of the LORD
Forever.

PSALM 23:6

Sufficiency

And God is able to make all grace abound toward you,
that you, always having all sufficiency in all things,
may have an abundance for every good work.

2 CORINTHIANS 9:8

And my God shall supply all your need
according to His riches in glory by Christ Jesus.

PHILIPPIANS 4:19

Therefore I say to you, whatever things
you ask when you pray, believe that you receive them,
and you will have them.

MARK 11:24

And He said to me, "My grace is sufficient for you,
for My strength is made perfect in weakness."
Therefore most gladly I will rather
boast in my infirmities, that the power of Christ
may rest upon me.

2 CORINTHIANS 12:9

Sufficiency

And in that day you will ask Me nothing.
Most assuredly, I say to you, whatever you ask the
Father in My name He will give you.
Until now you have asked nothing in My name.
Ask, and you will receive, that your joy may be full.

JOHN 16:23–24

Bless the LORD, O my soul,
And forget not all His benefits:
Who forgives all your iniquities,
Who heals all your diseases,
Who redeems your life from destruction,
Who crowns you with lovingkindness
and tender mercies,
Who satisfies your mouth with good things,
So that your youth is renewed
like the eagle's.

PSALM 103:2–5

Sufficiency

As His divine power has given to us all things that pertain to life and godliness, through the knowledge of Him who called us by glory and virtue, by which have been given to us exceedingly great and precious promises, that through these you may be partakers of the divine nature, having escaped the corruption that is in the world through lust.

2 PETER 1:3–4

God's Promises about Christian Growth. . .

Committing Your Life to Christ

That if you confess with your mouth the Lord Jesus and believe in your heart that God has raised Him from the dead, you will be saved. For with the heart one believes unto righteousness, and with the mouth confession is made unto salvation. For the Scripture says, "Whoever believes on Him will not be put to shame." For there is no distinction between Jew and Greek, for the same Lord over all is rich to all who call upon Him. For "whoever calls on the name of the LORD shall be saved."

ROMANS 10:9–13

Seek the LORD while He may be found,
Call upon Him while He is near.
Let the wicked forsake his way,
And the unrighteous man his thoughts;
Let him return to the LORD,
And He will have mercy on him;
And to our God,
For He will abundantly pardon.

ISAIAH 55:6–7

Committing Your Life to Christ

Behold, I stand at the door and knock.
If anyone hears My voice and opens the door,
I will come in to him and dine with him,
and he with Me.

REVELATION 3:20

All that the Father gives Me will come to Me,
and the one who comes to Me I will by no means cast
out. . . . And this is the will of Him who sent Me,
that everyone who sees the Son and
believes in Him may have everlasting life; and I will
raise him up at the last day. . . . No one can come to Me
unless the Father who sent Me draws him;
and I will raise him up at the last day. It is written in
the prophets, "And they shall all be taught by God."
Therefore everyone who has heard and learned from the
Father comes to Me. Not that anyone has seen
the Father, except He who is from God;
He has seen the Father. Most assuredly, I say to you,
he who believes in Me has everlasting life.

JOHN 6:37, 40

Committing Your Life to Christ

But without faith it is impossible to please Him,
for he who comes to God must believe that He is, and
that He is a rewarder of those who diligently seek Him.

HEBREWS 11:6

The Lord is not slack concerning His promise, as some
count slackness, but is longsuffering toward us,
not willing that any should perish but that all should
come to repentance. . . . but grow in the grace
and knowledge of our Lord and Savior Jesus Christ.
To Him be the glory both now and forever. Amen.

2 PETER 3:9, 18

Jesus answered and said to her, "Whoever drinks
of this water will thirst again, but whoever drinks of the
water that I shall give him will never thirst.
But the water that I shall give him will become in him a
fountain of water springing up into everlasting life."
The woman said to Him, "Sir, give me this water,
that I may not thirst, nor come here to draw."

JOHN 4:13–15

Beloved, do not believe every spirit, but test the spirits, whether they are of God; because many false prophets have gone out into the world. By this you know the Spirit of God: Every spirit that confesses that Jesus Christ has come in the flesh is of God, and every spirit that does not confess that Jesus Christ has come in the flesh is not of God. And this is the spirit of the Antichrist, which you have heard was coming, and is now already in the world.

1 JOHN 4:1-3

Come to Me, all you who labor and are heavy laden, and I will give you rest.

MATTHEW 11:28

Standing Against Worldliness

No one can serve two masters; for either
he will hate the one and love the other,
or else he will be loyal to the one and despise the other.
You cannot serve God and mammon.

MATTHEW 6:24

Do not love the world or the things in the world.
If anyone loves the world, the love of the Father is not
in him. For all that is in the world—the lust of
the flesh, the lust of the eyes, and the pride of life—
is not of the Father but is of the world.
And the world is passing away, and the lust of it;
but he who does the will of God abides forever.

1 JOHN 2:15–17

And do not be conformed to this world,
but be transformed by the renewing of your mind,
that you may prove what is that
good and acceptable and perfect will of God.

ROMANS 12:2

Standing Against Worldliness

And do this, knowing the time, that now it is high time to awake out of sleep; for now our salvation is nearer than when we first believed. The night is far spent, the day is at hand. Therefore let us cast off the works of darkness, and let us put on the armor of light. Let us walk properly, as in the day, not in revelry and drunkenness, not in lewdness and lust, not in strife and envy. But put on the Lord Jesus Christ, and make no provision for the flesh, to fulfill its lusts.

ROMANS 13:11–14

Then He said to them all, "If anyone desires to come after Me, let him deny himself, and take up his cross daily, and follow Me. For whoever desires to save his life will lose it, but whoever loses his life for My sake will save it. For what profit is it to a man if he gains the whole world, and is himself destroyed or lost?"

LUKE 9:23–25

Standing Against Worldliness

By which have been given to us exceedingly great and precious promises, that through these you may be partakers of the divine nature, having escaped the corruption that is in the world through lust.

2 PETER 1:4

But take heed to yourselves,
lest your hearts be weighed down with carousing,
drunkenness, and cares of this life,
and that Day come on you unexpectedly.

LUKE 21:34

Beloved, I beg you as sojourners and pilgrims,
abstain from fleshly lusts which war against the soul,
having your conduct honorable among the Gentiles,
that when they speak against you as evildoers,
they may, by your good works which they observe,
glorify God in the day of visitation.

1 PETER 2:11–12

Overcoming Lust

Now therefore, listen to me, my children;
Pay attention to the words of my mouth:
Do not let your heart turn aside to her ways,
Do not stray into her paths;
For she has cast down many wounded,
And all who were slain by her were strong men.
Her house is the way to hell,
Descending to the chambers of death.

PROVERBS 7:24–27

I say then: Walk in the Spirit, and you shall not fulfill the lust of the flesh. For the flesh lusts against the Spirit, and the Spirit against the flesh; and these are contrary to one another, so that you do not do the things that you wish.

GALATIANS 5:16–17

Overcoming Lust

That you put off, concerning your former conduct,
the old man which grows corrupt according
to the deceitful lusts, and be renewed in the spirit
of your mind, and that you put on the new man which
was created according to God, in true righteousness
and holiness. . . . nor give place to the devil.

EPHESIANS 4:22–24, 27

Do not lust after her beauty in your heart,
Nor let her allure you with her eyelids.
For by means of a harlot
A man is reduced to a crust of bread;
And an adulteress will prey upon his precious life.

PROVERBS 6:25–26

Overcoming Lust

Do you not know that your bodies are members of Christ? Shall I then take the members of Christ and make them members of a harlot? Certainly not! Or do you not know that he who is joined to a harlot is one body with her? For "the two," He says, "shall become one flesh." But he who is joined to the Lord is one spirit with Him. Flee sexual immorality. Every sin that a man does is outside the body, but he who commits sexual immorality sins against his own body. Or do you not know that your body is the temple of the Holy Spirit who is in you, whom you have from God, and you are not your own? For you were bought at a price; therefore glorify God in your body and in your spirit, which are God's.

1 CORINTHIANS 6:15–20

Setting Aside Pride

Pride goes before destruction,
And a haughty spirit before a fall.
Better to be of a humble spirit with the lowly,
Than to divide the spoil with the proud.
He who heeds the word wisely will find good,
And whoever trusts in the LORD, happy is he.

PROVERBS 16:18–20

He who is of a proud heart stirs up strife,
But he who trusts in the LORD will be prospered.
He who trusts in his own heart is a fool,
But whoever walks wisely will be delivered.

PROVERBS 28:25–26

Then Jesus called a little child to Him, set him in the midst of them, and said, "Assuredly, I say to you, unless you are converted and become as little children, you will by no means enter the kingdom of heaven. Therefore whoever humbles himself as this little child is the greatest in the kingdom of heaven."

MATTHEW 18:2–4

Setting Aside Pride

But He gives more grace. Therefore He says:
"God resists the proud,
But gives grace to the humble."
Therefore submit to God.
Resist the devil and he will flee from you.

JAMES 4:6–7

Humble yourselves in the sight of the Lord,
and He will lift you up.

JAMES 4:10

Whoever desires to become great among you,
let him be your servant.
And whoever desires to be first among you,
let him be your slave.

MATTHEW 20:26–27

Setting Aside Pride

Hear and give ear:
Do not be proud,
For the LORD has spoken.
Give glory to the LORD your God
Before He causes darkness,
And before your feet stumble
On the dark mountains,
And while you are looking for light,
He turns it into the shadow of death
And makes it dense darkness.
But if you will not hear it,
My soul will weep in secret for your pride;
My eyes will weep bitterly
And run down with tears,
Because the LORD's flock has been taken captive.

JEREMIAH 13:15–17

Take My yoke upon you and learn from Me,
for I am gentle and lowly in heart,
and you will find rest for your souls.
For My yoke is easy and My burden is light.

MATTHEW 11:29–30

Choosing to Speak Carefully

Death and life are in the power of the tongue,
And those who love it will eat its fruit.

PROVERBS 18:21

Let no corrupt word proceed out of your mouth, but what is good for necessary edification, that it may impart grace to the hearers. . . . Let all bitterness, wrath, anger, clamor, and evil speaking be put away from you, with all malice. And be kind to one another, tenderhearted, forgiving one another, even as God in Christ forgave you.

EPHESIANS 4:29, 31–32

Pleasant words are like a honeycomb,
Sweetness to the soul and health to the bones.

PROVERBS 16:24

He who guards his mouth preserves his life,
But he who opens wide his lips shall have destruction.

PROVERBS 13:3

Choosing to Speak Carefully

A good man out of the good treasure of his heart brings forth good; and an evil man out of the evil treasure of his heart brings forth evil. For out of the abundance of the heart his mouth speaks.

LUKE 6:45

But I say to you that for every idle word men may speak, they will give account of it in the day of judgment.

MATTHEW 12:36

Whoever guards his mouth and tongue
Keeps his soul from troubles.

PROVERBS 21:23

As long as my breath is in me,
And the breath of God in my nostrils,
My lips will not speak wickedness,
Nor my tongue utter deceit.

JOB 27:3–4

Keeping Centered in Christ

Let the word of Christ dwell in you richly in all wisdom, teaching and admonishing one another in psalms and hymns and spiritual songs, singing with grace in your hearts to the Lord. And whatever you do in word or deed, do all in the name of the Lord Jesus, giving thanks to God the Father through Him.

COLOSSIANS 3:16–17

I love those who love me,
And those who seek me diligently will find me.

PROVERBS 8:17

Seek the LORD and His strength;
Seek His face evermore!
Remember His marvelous works which He has done,
His wonders, and the judgments of His mouth.

1 CHRONICLES 16:11–12

Keeping Centered in Christ

You are My friends if you do whatever I command you.
No longer do I call you servants, for a servant
does not know what his master is doing; but I have
called you friends, for all things that I heard from
My Father I have made known to you.
You did not choose Me, but I chose you and
appointed you that you should go and bear fruit,
and that your fruit should remain, that whatever you
ask the Father in My name He may give you.

JOHN 15:14–16

I will bless the LORD at all times; His praise shall
continually be in my mouth.
My soul shall make its boast in the LORD;
The humble shall hear of it and be glad.
Oh, magnify the LORD with me,
And let us exalt His name together.
I sought the LORD, and He heard me,
And delivered me from all my fears.

PSALM 34:1–4

Keeping Centered in Christ

In You, O LORD, I put my trust;
Let me never be put to shame. . . .
For You are my hope, O Lord GOD;
You are my trust from my youth. . . .
Let my mouth be filled with Your praise
And with Your glory all the day.

PSALM 71:1, 5, 8

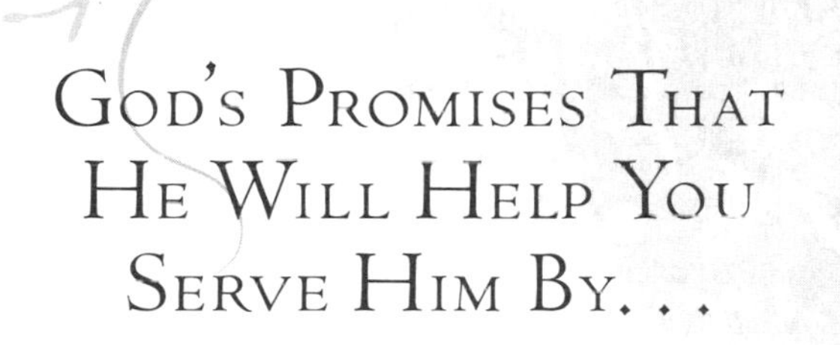

God's Promises That He Will Help You Serve Him By. . .

Praying Effectively

Be anxious for nothing, but in everything by prayer and supplication, with thanksgiving, let your requests be made known to God; and the peace of God, which surpasses all understanding, will guard your hearts and minds through Christ Jesus.

PHILIPPIANS 4:6–7

Assuredly, I say to you, whatever you bind on earth will be bound in heaven, and whatever you loose on earth will be loosed in heaven. Again I say to you that if two of you agree on earth concerning anything that they ask, it will be done for them by My Father in heaven.

MATTHEW 18:18–19

Confess your trespasses to one another, and pray for one another, that you may be healed.
The effective, fervent prayer of a righteous man avails much. Elijah was a man with a nature like ours, and he prayed earnestly that it would not rain; and it did not rain on the land for three years and six months. And he prayed again, and the heaven gave rain, and the earth produced its fruit.

JAMES 5:16–18

Praying Effectively

Call to Me, and I will answer you, and show
you great and mighty things, which you do not know.

JEREMIAH 33:3

So I say to you, ask, and it will be given to you; seek,
and you will find; knock, and it will be opened to you.

LUKE 11:9

And when you pray, you shall not be like
the hypocrites. For they love to pray standing in the
synagogues and on the corners of the streets,
that they may be seen by men. Assuredly, I say to you,
they have their reward. But you, when you pray, go into
your room, and when you have shut your door,
pray to your Father who is in the secret place; and your
Father who sees in secret will reward you openly.

MATTHEW 6:5–6

Evening and morning and at noon
I will pray, and cry aloud,
And He shall hear my voice.

PSALM 55:17

Witnessing Effectively

You are the light of the world. A city that is set on a hill cannot be hidden. Nor do they light a lamp and put it under a basket, but on a lampstand, and it gives light to all who are in the house. Let your light so shine before men, that they may see your good works and glorify your Father in heaven.

MATTHEW 5:14–16

No one, when he has lit a lamp, puts it in a secret place or under a basket, but on a lampstand, that those who come in may see the light.

LUKE 11:33

Praying always with all prayer and supplication in the Spirit, being watchful to this end with all perseverance and supplication for all the saints—and for me, that utterance may be given to me, that I may open my mouth boldly to make known the mystery of the gospel, for which I am an ambassador in chains; that in it I may speak boldly, as I ought to speak.

EPHESIANS 6:18–20

Witnessing Effectively

Finally, all of you be of one mind,
having compassion for one another; love as brothers,
be tenderhearted, be courteous; not returning
evil for evil or reviling for reviling, but on the contrary
blessing, knowing that you were called to this,
that you may inherit a blessing. For
"He who would love life
And see good days,
Let him refrain his tongue from evil,
And his lips from speaking deceit.
Let him turn away from evil and do good;
Let him seek peace and pursue it."

1 PETER 3:8–11

But sanctify the Lord God in your hearts,
and always be ready to give a defense to everyone who
asks you a reason for the hope that is in you,
with meekness and fear.

1 PETER 3:15

Witnessing Effectively

Also I say to you, whoever confesses Me before men,
him the Son of Man also will confess before
the angels of God. But he who denies Me before men
will be denied before the angels of God.

LUKE 12:8–9

Therefore do not be ashamed of the testimony
of our Lord, nor of me His prisoner, but share with me
in the sufferings for the gospel according to the
power of God, who has saved us and called us with a
holy calling, not according to our works,
but according to His own purpose and grace which was
given to us in Christ Jesus before time began,
but has now been revealed by the appearing of our
Savior Jesus Christ, who has abolished
death and brought life and immortality
to light through the gospel.

2 TIMOTHY 1:8–10

The fruit of the righteous is a tree of life,
And he who wins souls is wise.

PROVERBS 11:30

Understanding God's Will

The LORD will guide you continually,
And satisfy your soul in drought,
And strengthen your bones;
You shall be like a watered garden,
And like a spring of water, whose waters do not fail.
For you shall not go out with haste,
Nor go by flight;
For the LORD will go before you,
And the God of Israel will be your rear guard.

ISAIAH 58:11–12

I say to you that likewise there will be more joy in heaven over one sinner who repents than over ninety nine just persons who need no repentance.

LUKE 15:7

The Lord is not slack concerning His promise, as some count slackness, but is longsuffering toward us, not willing that any should perish but that all should come to repentance.

2 PETER 3:9

Understanding God's Will

He found him in a desert land
And in the wasteland, a howling wilderness;
He encircled him, He instructed him,
He kept him as the apple of His eye.
As an eagle stirs up its nest,
Hovers over its young,
Spreading out its wings, taking them up,
Carrying them on its wings,
So the LORD alone led him,
And there was no foreign god with him.

DEUTERONOMY 32:10–12

A man's heart plans his way,
But the LORD directs his steps. . . .
The lot is cast into the lap,
But its every decision is from the LORD.

PROVERBS 16:9, 33

Obeying God

That all the peoples of the earth may know that the LORD is God; there is no other. Let your heart therefore be loyal to the LORD our God, to walk in His statutes and keep His commandments, as at this day.

1 KINGS 8:60–61

Now therefore, if you will indeed obey My voice and keep My covenant, then you shall be a special treasure to Me above all people; for all the earth is Mine.

EXODUS 19:5

Do not be deceived, God is not mocked; for whatever a man sows, that he will also reap. For he who sows to his flesh will of the flesh reap corruption, but he who sows to the Spirit will of the Spirit reap everlasting life.

GALATIANS 6:7–8

Obeying God

Casting down arguments and every high thing that exalts itself against the knowledge of God, bringing every thought into captivity to the obedience of Christ.

2 CORINTHIANS 10:5

Behold, You desire truth in the inward parts,
And in the hidden part
You will make me to know wisdom.

PSALM 51:6

And the world is passing away, and the lust of it; but he who does the will of God abides forever.

1 JOHN 2:17

If anyone does not abide in Me, he is cast out as a branch and is withered; and they gather them and throw them into the fire, and they are burned. If you abide in Me, and My words abide in you, you will ask what you desire, and it shall be done for you. . . . If you keep My commandments, you will abide in My love, just as I have kept My Father's commandments and abide in His love.

JOHN 15:6–7, 10

Giving to God's Work

Do not lay up for yourselves treasures on earth, where moth and rust destroy and where thieves break in and steal; but lay up for yourselves treasures in heaven, where neither moth nor rust destroys and where thieves do not break in and steal. For where your treasure is, there your heart will be also.

MATTHEW 6:19–21

Now Jesus sat opposite the treasury and saw how the people put money into the treasury. And many who were rich put in much. Then one poor widow came and threw in two mites, which make a quadrans. So He called His disciples to Himself and said to them, "Assuredly, I say to you that this poor widow has put in more than all those who have given to the treasury; for they all put in out of their abundance, but she out of her poverty put in all that she had, her whole livelihood."

MARK 12:41–44

Giving to God's Work

But this I say: He who sows sparingly will also reap sparingly, and he who sows bountifully will also reap bountifully. So let each one give as he purposes in his heart, not grudgingly or of necessity; for God loves a cheerful giver.

2 CORINTHIANS 9:6–7

He who is faithful in what is least is faithful also in much; and he who is unjust in what is least is unjust also in much. Therefore if you have not been faithful in the unrighteous mammon, who will commit to your trust the true riches?

LUKE 16:10–11

He who has a generous eye will be blessed,
For he gives of his bread to the poor.

PROVERBS 22:9

Giving to God's Work

As soon as the commandment was circulated,
the children of Israel brought
in abundance the firstfruits of grain and wine,
oil and honey, and of all the produce of the field;
and they brought in abundantly the tithe of everything.

2 CHRONICLES 31:5

And let us not grow weary while doing good,
for in due season we shall reap if we do
not lose heart. Therefore, as we have opportunity,
let us to good to all, especially to those
who are of the household of faith.

GALATIANS 6:9-10

Give, and it will be given to you: good measure,
pressed down, shaken together, and running over
will be put into your bosom. For with the
same measure that you use, it will be
measured back to you.

LUKE 6:38

Reading God's Word

For the word of God is living and powerful,
and sharper than any two–edged sword,
piercing even to the division of soul and spirit, and of
joints and marrow, and is a discerner
of the thoughts and intents of the heart.

HEBREWS 4:12

Your word I have hidden in my heart,
That I might not sin against You. . . .
I will delight myself in Your statutes;
I will not forget Your word.

PSALM 119:11, 16

How sweet are Your words to my taste,
Sweeter than honey to my mouth!
Through Your precepts I get understanding;
Therefore I hate every false way.
Your word is a lamp to my feet
And a light to my path.

PSALM 119:103–105

Reading God's Word

Remove from me the way of lying,
And grant me Your law graciously.
I have chosen the way of truth;
Your judgments I have laid before me.

PSALM 119:29–30

But He answered and said,
"It is written, 'Man shall not live by bread alone,
but by every word that proceeds
from the mouth of God.'"

MATTHEW 4:4

Heaven and earth will pass away,
but My words will by no means pass away.

LUKE 21:33

Your words were found, and I ate them;
And Your word was to me the joy
and rejoicing of my heart;
For I am called by Your name,
O LORD God of hosts.

JEREMIAH 15:16

Reading God's Word

Having been born again, not of corruptible seed
but incorruptible, through the word of God
which lives and abides forever, because
"All flesh is as grass,
And all the glory of man as the flower of the grass.
The grass withers,
And its flower falls away,
But the word of the LORD endures forever."
Now this is the word which by the gospel
was preached to you.

1 PETER 1:23–25

It is the Spirit who gives life;
the flesh profits nothing.
The words that I speak to you are spirit,
and they are life.

JOHN 6:63

GOD'S PROMISES THAT HE'LL HELP YOU SERVE HIM BY . . .

Walking With Christ

Abide in Me, and I in you. As the branch cannot bear
fruit of itself, unless it abides in the vine,
neither can you, unless you abide in Me. I am the vine,
you are the branches. He who abides in Me,
and I in him, bears much fruit; for without Me you can
do nothing. If anyone does not abide in Me,
he is cast out as a branch and is withered;
and they gather them and throw them into the fire,
and they are burned. If you abide in Me,
and My words abide in you, you will ask what you
desire, and it shall be done for you.

JOHN 15:4–7

And now, little children, abide in Him,
that when He appears, we may have confidence and
not be ashamed before Him at His coming.

1 JOHN 2:28

A fool's mouth is his destruction,
And his lips are the snare of his soul.

PROVERBS 18:7

Walking With Christ

Let the word of Christ dwell in you richly in
all wisdom, teaching and admonishing one another
in psalms and hymns and spiritual songs,
singing with grace in your hearts to the Lord.

COLOSSIANS 3:16

Now by this we know that we know Him, if we keep
His commandments. He who says, "I know Him,"
and does not keep His commandments, is a liar,
and the truth is not in him. But whoever keeps His word,
truly the love of God is perfected in him. By this
we know that we are in Him. He who says he abides in
Him ought himself also to walk just as He walked.

1 JOHN 2:3–6

Blessed is the man who listens to me,
Watching daily at my gates,
Waiting at the posts of my doors.

PROVERBS 8:34

But be doers of the word, and not hearers only,
deceiving yourselves.

JAMES 1:22

Building Your Faith

Now faith is the substance of things hoped for,
the evidence of things not seen. . . .
By faith we understand that the worlds were framed
by the word of God, so that the things which
are seen were not made of things which are visible. . . .
But without faith it is impossible to please Him,
for he who comes to God must believe that He is,
and that He is a rewarder of those who
diligently seek Him. . . . By faith he forsook Egypt,
not fearing the wrath of the king;
for he endured as seeing Him who is invisible.

HEBREWS 11: 1, 3, 6, 27

That the genuineness of your faith,
being much more precious than gold that perishes,
though it is tested by fire, may be found to praise,
honor, and glory at the revelation of Jesus Christ,
whom having not seen you love. Though now you do
not see Him, yet believing, you rejoice with joy
inexpressible and full of glory, receiving the end
of your faith—the salvation of your souls.

1 PETER 1:7–9

Building Your Faith

With God nothing will be impossible.

LUKE 1:37

If any of you lacks wisdom, let him ask of God, who gives to all liberally and without reproach, and it will be given to him. But let him ask in faith, with no doubting, for he who doubts is like a wave of the sea driven and tossed by the wind. For let not that man suppose that he will receive anything from the Lord; he is a double-minded man, unstable in all his ways.

JAMES 1:5–8

He did not waver at the promise of God through unbelief, but was strengthened in faith, giving glory to God, and being fully convinced that what He had promised He was also able to perform.

ROMANS 4:20–21

Building Your Faith

We are hard-pressed on every side, yet not crushed;
we are perplexed, but not in despair; persecuted,
but not forsaken; struck down,
but not destroyed—always carrying about in
the body the dying of the Lord Jesus, that the life of
Jesus also may be manifested in our body.

2 CORINTHIANS 4:8–10

Keep yourselves in the love of God, looking for the
mercy of our Lord Jesus Christ unto eternal life.
And on some have compassion, making a distinction;
but others save with fear, pulling them out of the fire,
hating even the garment defiled by the flesh.
Now to Him who is able to keep you from stumbling,
And to present you faultless
Before the presence of His glory with exceeding joy,
To God our Savior,
Who alone is wise,
Be glory and majesty,
Dominion and power,
Both now and forever.
Amen.

JUDE 1:21–24

God's Plan of Salvation...

For all have sinned and fall short of the glory of God.

ROMANS 3:23

But God demonstrates His own love toward us,
in that while we were still sinners, Christ died for us.

ROMANS 5:8

Therefore, just as through one man sin entered
the world, and death through sin, and thus death
spread to all men, because all sinned.

ROMANS 5:12

For the wages of sin is death, but the gift of God
is eternal life in Christ Jesus our Lord.

ROMANS 6:23

For God did not send His Son into the world
to condemn the world, but that the world through Him
might be saved. . . . He who believes in the Son
has everlasting life; and he who does not believe the Son
shall not see life, but the wrath of God abides on him.

JOHN 3:17, 36

Moreover, brethren, I declare to you the gospel which I preached to you, which also you received and in which you stand, by which also you are saved, if you hold fast that word which I preached to you—unless you believed in vain. For I delivered to you first of all that which I also received: that Christ died for our sins according to the Scriptures, and that He was buried, and that He rose again the third day according to the Scriptures.

1 CORINTHIANS 15:1–4

For God so loved the world that He gave His only begotten Son, that whoever believes in Him should not perish but have everlasting life.

JOHN 3:16

For by grace you have been saved through faith, and that not of yourselves; it is the gift of God, not of works, lest anyone should boast.

EPHESIANS 2:8–9

But what does it say? "The word is near you, in your mouth and in your heart" (that is, the word of faith which we preach): that if you confess with your mouth the Lord Jesus and believe in your heart that God has raised Him from the dead, you will be saved. For with the heart one believes unto righteousness, and with the mouth confession is made unto salvation.

ROMANS 10:8–10

Therefore whoever confesses Me before men, him I will also confess before My Father who is in heaven.

MATTHEW 10:32

Behold, I stand at the door and knock. If anyone hears My voice and opens the door, I will come in to him and dine with him, and he with Me.

REVELATION 3:20

Dear God,
I admit I've sinned and fallen short of Your glory.
I realize the penalty for my sin is death, and I believe
it was paid by the shed blood of Jesus Christ.
I'm willing to repent of my sins,
and I now confess Christ as my Savior
and make Him the Lord of my life.
In Jesus' Name, Amen.

NOTES